Aι

THE BOOK OF WINTER

THE BOOK OF WINTER

Winner of the
1988 Ohio State
University Press / *The Journal*
Award in Poetry

Sue Owen

Ohio State University Press • Columbus

ACKNOWLEDGMENTS

My thanks to my parents, my friends, and especially to Thomas Owen for his support and helpful criticism.

Grateful acknowledgment is made for permission to reprint here poems that have appeared in the following periodicals and anthologies: *Harvard Magazine* for "The Little Flies"; *The Iowa Review* for "Bone Soup," "Tattletale," "My Graveyard Poem," "Recipe for Night," and "Cat in the Corner"; *Kayak* for "Zero"; *The Massachusetts Review* for "The Pull of Gravity"; *The Nation* for "The Owl"; *The New Orleans Review* for "Needlework" and "A Rolling Pin Poem"; *North American Review* for "The Prophecy of Ink"; *Ploughshares* for "Leading the Blind," "The Wolf," and "My Name Is Snow"; *Poetry* for "The White Rabbit"; *Poetry Northwest* for "Blood Relatives"; *Poetry Now* for "The North Star"; *The Southern Review* for "The Squirrels," "Fortune Teller," "Idle Hands," "Pain Is Certain," and "Chilled to the Bone"; *The Virginia Quarterly Review* for "Hatred" and "Playing Dead"; *Anthology of Magazine Verse* for "The Owl," "Leading the Blind," "Hatred," "My Graveyard Poem," and "The White Rabbit"; and *Woman Poet: The South* for "The Book of Winter."

The Book of Winter was also a finalist at the Associated Writing Programs competition and is an AWP Award Series Selection.

Owen, Sue
    The book of winter / Sue Owen.
        p.   cm.
    "Winner of the 1988 Ohio State University Press / *The Journal* award in poetry."
    ISBN 0–8142–0474–0. ISBN 0–8142–0475–9 (pbk.)
    I. Title.
PS3565.W564B66 1988   88–19489
811'.54—dc19   CIP

Printed in the U.S.A.

⊗

Listen to the wind,
how it will blow
even its heart out
to make you cold.

CONTENTS

I

II

III

IV

V

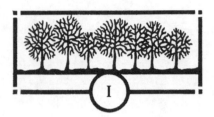

I

ZERO

This is the story of zero,
born to live a life
of emptiness, only
child of plus and minus.

Its bones invisible
so it could be seen through
like an eye.
With that vision, you could

see the past and future
and how they mimic each other.
At first, it was thought
the zero was a mouth

and would say something
profound to the numbers.
But added to them, it never
amounted to much, and

subtracted, it never wanted
to take anything away.
Zero was a sad case,
only wanted to master emotion

and silence like chess.
Each winter, the approaching
degrees never could locate
its cold, missing heart.

THE WHITE RABBIT

You practice death
like this.
You wear your own ghost.
In the white snow,
you welcome your disguise.

You let the wind
blow through you
on its way to breaking twigs
for firewood.
You let the wind push
you as the snow leans
in fright against a house.

Winter wants to settle
your life in this cold.
A dispute it has
against your fur that fits,
against your heart's heat.

Already the earth
has given up its shape to
the falling snow.
You, too, should give up
the randomness of your paw
prints that makes
the hunter stop and wonder.

Already one bullet in his
gun belongs to your body.
Your dark eyes will learn
that when light
abandons them, the stew pot
had heard about you,
and luck was waiting for
your one loose foot.

RECIPE FOR NIGHT

All the ingredients share
the same purpose.
Put in the stars
where the darkness
was blinded by light.
Their sighs can be heard
from great distances,
like a flavor.

And put in the moon
when it is a full cup.
That pure light is better
than any milk.

You can see your dreams
with it.
You can hear what
the sun whispers to it,
what the other side
of the earth won't yet tell.

What else can we put in?
Don't forget the darkness
hurrying to be remembered.
It leans into this
stirring like a close shadow,
like a wind out to make
trouble for the leaves.

So put in a pinch of
darkness, spoon of darkness,
dash of darkness; it's
all the same.
Night turns out the same,
even if the moon closes
its eye, even if
the stars shine breathless.

HEAVEN AND EARTH

Think of dust's plight.
It drifts halfway
between heaven and earth
and cannot decide.

The wind tries to think
for it, but the dust
settles anyway
where it is not wanted.

It settles in the house
to silence the books
and tables with a sleep.
To turn the room
into the gray business
of a dream to which
the cobwebs
from their corners gesture.

To which the spiders
come down from the air
and witness.
And the dust grows more
sure in the stillness.
It closes the eye
of the mirror and closes
the vision of the windows
until time turns away.

This is what the dust
must have wanted.
It remembered how the dead
kept calling, and on
its way to them chose earth.

TATTLETALE

T told A that it
was a man or a scarecrow
and terror was its passion.
A passed this on to TT

and fear doubled its earnings.
T and T could point
in four directions like
a center, and from it

their tongues blew until
L knew what was up.
And L, leaning into the sound,
was not one to hold secrets.

It believed in word of mouth
like a religion.
L, the inventor of lullaby
and language, passed

the story of fear on to E,
the way a message is
slipped, quiet as a whisper,
under a closed door.

And E, the author of end
or eternity, passed fear on
so the T of this tale knew
the breath of ancestry.

Fear is as thick as blood.
And T told everything
to fill the ears of
the little ones, A, L, and E.

MY NAME IS SNOW

I want to report to you
that in my name, SUE
ANN OWEN, I have found
the word SNOW.
I can also spell out,
without much trouble,
the animals that
dare to live there, SWAN,
EWE, and that old SOW,
though the SNOW
makes it quite cold for them.
This is not to mention
the NOSE that lives
there in my cold name,
taking in and out for me,
I suppose, the necessary breath.
And that a SAW in there
saws when I sleep, and
there is NEWS, and the ONE
SUN that does not WANE.
And other words
that want me to USE them NOW,
like SEE and SEW,
NONE and NO, and SANE.
And WE and AWE.
I haven't used them all up.
And for good reason I
don't mention
the ones I've rejected,
like NUN and NEON.
But one of my favorites I
OWN rhymes with SNOW, is WOE.
I also want to report that
without rearranging my letters,
my name backwards or
upside down means nothing.

8

THE OWL

It's his eyes
that you can't forget.
He is seeing through
darkness to the death
of a mouse.
He doesn't breathe, blink.

His claws have locked
him onto a branch.
He is wearing a coat
of feathers to hide
the turn of his thoughts.
All the trees
here become skeletons.
Only their shadows bow.

The gravity in his heart
is pulling the forest
closer so he can
focus on the smallness.
A toad inside
his stomach is, at last,
turning into an acid.

This is how the owl's
mind must turn.
This is how it is
to be so awake the mind
is too large for a skull,
eyes almost lidless.

The intensity of the will
burning down
to the hottest coal.
His eyes set the forest
on fire, the dark fire
that even the moonlight
cannot put out.

THE BOOK OF WINTER

There's so much
snow in the book of winter.
The table of contents
is filled with it;
you look hard to see.
But it's a white world
marred by the tracks
of squirrels and sparrows,
little animals in
a hurry to say nothing.

There are nuts
and seeds they want to
find, something hidden.
And those rabbits
whose bodies are white
are almost invisible laying
down their soft track.
Their little marks
are the zeroes adding up.

The landscape of the first
page is entirely white,
so all the meaning
can be hidden, the dead
grass, dead leaves.
The sun shines palely,
as if it had seen a ghost.

Only the hard, red
berries in the bushes
dare to speak of survival.
Sometimes here the voices
of the dead come back,
reaching through the snow,
carried like a thin
narrative in the wind.

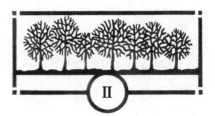

II

THE NORTH STAR

See, it is the only one
that will not lie.
It is not tempted
to change like the others

that flicker to color
and disappear.
It has seen so much it knows
better than that.

It remembers the frailties
of being human
and becoming lost, all those
drowned ones it saw,

begging to the end for air,
or those claimed by
the woods who never again
would hear the human voice.

This star is the only one
that knows the importance
of position
in the flow of time and weather.

And that if you want
salvation, you will
look to it as the others did
and not ask it why.

CHILLED TO THE BONE

It is winter now
and time for the wind to
tell you a cold tale.
It knows how to chill
your bones just by blowing
your way, just by making
the shutters of your house flap,
though nothing is
so lucky as to fly away.
Don't be afraid now
when the wind starts to howl.
It will tell you what it did
to the others, the trees,
how it scared their
leaves away, and scared
away the green of grass until
it was brown and pale.
And how the pond now
is as lifeless as a mirror
and you could see your face
there in that ice.
And the rest of the land lies
dead around it, at last,
ready for the first snow.
Don't be afraid now
if the wind tells you of death.
All of this is just a tale
made out of cold breath,
and you know
that words cannot hurt you,
even if in this unfinished
tale, the wind blows
your window open and blows
your roaring fire out.

THE ONION POEM

Not another onion poem
to make you weep.
Not to tell you about
the sorrow in
the onion's heart, layers
and layers of it.

The onion that must have
known what death,
poverty, and disease
can add up to.
Or, heartbreak, that can
hurt more than the edge
of the paring knife.

How long the onion waited
in the earth, collecting
the rumors of pain,
we do not know.
Or, if it was fed by
what the rainwater had seen.

But now the onion sits
before us in its coat
of brown skin,
a fat witness, ready
to let us see the truth
it has brought.

There always was a price
to pay for such knowledge.
And if we weep, there
is nothing the onion can do
to comfort us.

15

I DOT MY I

I dot my I with ink.
I dot my I in the dark
words that are my birth and life.

Once I was the dot
in the I of the word desire.
My breath was the dot

of the first penny I spent.
But now I dot the dark
word that is my brain.

It is the dark dot of thought
that spins above my spine.
I dot the dark smallness

I am in the words
universe and mortality.
And, at night, I look up

from this dark dot of earth
to see the dots of stars
that connect everything

to the same story of smallness.
I am the speck in the word spectacle.
I am the small dot

in the word nothing
that is easily overlooked.
I am just another dot

rolled on the dice of fate.
So I dot the river
of my sorrow with one more pebble.

I dot the pain of this
knowledge of my smallness
with one small, dark tear.

FORTUNE TELLER

Here is the crystal ball
that like an eye
will look for us.
It will look to the birth

and the death and in between.
It will look through
time because time
after all is invisible.

Any object in its way,
bones and breath,
will give up everything if
the right question is asked.

And your life is the question.
Now you open your wrinkled
palm and show
the lines that cross and

hurt each other on their way.
How can I untwist the wind
that blew you here?
How can I say

that what you want, you
and your shadow must share?
But there always will be
enough of the sadness.

IDLE HANDS

How do you know
when the devil has taken
charge, makes devil's work?
What will it mean

when your hands gesture
differently, but they
don't speak of hunger?
The new alphabet of needs

takes over as
a shadow sometimes looms
larger than a body at dusk?
Then will you be accountable?

Then will the occurrences
come from orders
your brain didn't send down?
And it won't be what

your blood wanted, or
your bones that are illiterate?
I'm speaking to you
who want answers, whose

hands grip this book, or
whose hands listen in a lap.
What must the devil intend
to need your hands?

THE DEVIL MAKES DO

The devil's job isn't easy,
but then it's not hard either.
Everyone knows the job
is this: how to send

a worm into the apple
of the heart to start up
the rot, and rot the soul
until it stinks to hell.

And what is that little worm
the devil uses but wrong?
Everything in the world
that goes wrong.

Wrong working its way
through the world as money,
working its way as dice
and also as liquor.

Everyone knows that making
wrong work is
a tireless job, and the devil
must work late hours.

But why should the devil complain,
though his job is thankless,
if disease, war, and murder
want to help him out?

Everyone knows that
the devil's take-home pay
isn't great, but, that hell,
at least it is a living.

THE PROPHECY OF INK

The night has provided
enough ink to write,
so I must write.

I write to this hour
and its traveling minutes.
I make an address to
the infinity in my clock.

I write to this chair
that never woke up
from its perpetual dream.
In it, it holds my weight.

To this patient table
that feels my thoughts
written upon it, I write.
I write as a bird can
write only to sky.

I write to this breath
of air that was just mine.
I am writing my blood's
best farewell to this
paper, even to this pen.

Then I must write to what
I have already written.
I will say to it:

These words possessed me.
Ink was only the shadow
of what I meant to say.
In the life that comes,
this darkness stays.

LITANY FOR ICE

Ice, you are death's
blood in the veins
of winter.

Ice, you are the turned
key in winter's heart.
And that heart is shut.

Ice, you are the mirror
that ragged trees
must see themselves in.

Ice, you are the stiff
hand that stops
a great river's running.

Ice, you despise summer.

Ice, instead the north
sends its winds
to bow to your zeroes.

Ice, you dress in
the difficult crystal that
diamonds try to wear.

Ice, you are the twinkle
in the eye of crisis.
Your thoughts
are smooth and flawless,
like the grip of logic.

Ice, in winter's brain
your plan for the end
of the world is perfect.

Ice, it is cold and clear.

LEADING THE BLIND

I will lead you
with my dark eyes.
My eyes of ash, shadow, earth.
My eyes that are secrets

the darkness keeps
and never gives back.
This is the season of night.
It is the landscape

of sleep, dreams, and death.
We will not talk to
the features of the moon.
There is no way to complete

the light that starts stars.
Even the heart can show
its hidden form.
And the random world

will receive us as it falls
into the nearest shapes.
You will follow me
as an alphabet follows sound,

blind to what light imagines.
These words, these syllables
of the dark, will
be your reliable guide.

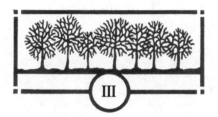

III

THE TRICK OF THE SKULL

Believe in me now.
I am the magician in black.
Be sure to notice
how my hands touch this skull.

I am placing it here
before us on the table.
It will talk to us.
You must believe that death

was always this near.
This skull thinks for the dead.
There is so much they
still want to say.

And language never dies,
although in these dark sockets
the eyes burn out, and
no nose invites in breath.

Believe in this skull.
You will hear now the thoughts
that haunt the labyrinth
of its brain.

You will hear the bare teeth
jump again in the cold.
They will click once for no.
Click twice for yes.

25

HATRED

If H is a house on fire,
flame is the merciless dance.
But the A, next to it,
contradicts.

It is the A of water,
of pails and tears.
It is the A of quarrel.
Day and night have not yet

ended their disagreement
and neither have the A and
the belligerent T.
T must be a no if A is yes.

Or, they could be stillness
and breath
staring each other down.
And R next to them would not

call off its planned malice.
This is the R of war,
rage, and roar, on its way
to break up the dreams of E.

And the E of energy will
unleash three tongues,
its pitchfork, against the D.
D is not the D of dead.

It is the D of demon, knows
poison and power,
so that inside this word,
HATRED never freezes over.

BLOOD RELATIVES

We'll let the knife
introduce itself,
the sharp shine in its smile.
It can cut for us
a slice of bread, some
pig that squeals.
Where the knife goes,
the lips of a wound confess.

Not to leave out
the nail, the thorn in
the side of lumber.
The hammer in hand
intends a direction for it,
but the nail escapes.
It is a convict, goes
looking for trouble, lockjaw.

Shard of glass
belongs in this album.
Its heart a mirror
shattered on the floor.
It knows splintering pain.
It wants revenge,
a place to nestle,
to bed down in soft flesh.

And we won't forget scissors.

And we won't forget needle
stuck in the pin
cushion and not talking.
No thread following it.
It plans a way to prick.
It has one drop
of your meek blood in mind.

A DEDICATION

I dedicate this poem
to the tree
that lent its body to my voice.
I want to remember for it

the passing of time,
how the sky, a concept,
was mostly blue and endless,
and the sun burned

each day to light the way
for sight.
The birds that stopped by
and perched, not meaning

to interrupt
the silent thought of growth.
Leaves that turned
into themselves and let go.

28

I want to respect this tree
that let so many seasons
harm and heal as change will do.
The wind and rain

for their reasons coming
to it, right or wrong.
The lightning that knew
how to locate the worst pain.

PAIN IS CERTAIN

I am your pain.
Your nerves are on my map.
Your fears, too,
I can locate in the confusion

of sorrow and sickness.
I can take my time,
as old age does, on my way,
delay, linger wherever

I am not wanted, but
the stars will rise and set
in their sockets,
looking out for me.

Nevertheless, I am on my way,
like a conclusion
so obvious I am not drawn.
And if I digress now,

because talk explains while
it distracts, that is
because I am so close
I can see your blood running.

And I can see it better
when, with this flame,
I light those
frail candles you call bones.

THE POISONED APPLE

Snow White, I want
to explain everything
from this green
tree where I still hang
on the bough.

I want you to know
that this shape I am
is what the sun taught.
I had to learn this
trick of shine, this red
that is my destiny.

Neither you nor I
know why the wind whispers
about a mirror that
tries to lie, or can
imagine a story we could
make up about jealousy.

But I know one day,
a ladder and a hand
could come to pick me.
Any queen who wanted to
take me, because
she hates, could dip my
one-half into a poison.

It is fate that my
prettiness and sweetness
will draw someone close,
until the bite.
I want to explain this
now, if I am that
apple, that red period
that will stop your life.

THE GLASS COFFIN

Now you sleep
the pretty death.
Snow White, the poisoned
apple you bit is
caught in your throat.

Snow White, your body
is like your name now,
thick with a cold
that grips you.
Your blue eyes return no
knowing when looked in.

You must be dreaming
that blankness of winter.
Snow White,
it must be a place
of few stars and great
air, where movement is
always only a wind.

And your two hands, that
cannot remember what
they held, must lie
empty like birds' nests.
Your arms emptied
themselves of holding too,
like trees that drop
their bleeding leaves.

Snow White, you
are a child of sleep and
loneliness.
The days come and breath
steps its way, slowly,
through you, because
someone wants you and will
melt your lips of ice.

A QUILT

Nothing now, but sleep,
and this quilt above you
to keep you warm.
Nothing now, but the darkness

and the cold,
and the dreams to come,
in which the world you
remember is forgotten.

But the world is still here,
stitched into this quilt.
Even if you forget it,
the needle stitched in breath,

and the heartbeat,
and the rush of blood
that leads to memory.
Even the tick of time is here,

so that everything here
that repeats itself
leads to the world's patterns.
And the needle named

everything it saw with the stitch,
the stones, roads, stars,
the rivers and mountains
stitched into the earth

of this cloth, so there
would never be an emptiness.
So there would never be
the loneliness of nothing.

THE LITTLE FLIES

Why not now?
You buzz that question.
You buzz the room.
You buzz the stillness

to an irritation.
You buzz to harm
the windowpane until it breaks
and lets you out.

And you buzz because
the light keeps calling.
To anyone the world out there
looks real enough,

even through glass where
the wind still blows cold
and the snow
fills up the lost spaces.

Little flies, even if
you buzz that question again,
time will not hear you.
Time is invisible

and far away planning its tricks.
You can buzz your
body to death or wait for
the slow gift of summer.

KNIFE BLADE

I want to be more
than the author of death.
I want to write their
story with the spilt blood.

To tell about the cut
throat of the goose
as it trickles
onto the white innocence

of the feathers.
To tell how the pig's final
fatness leads it to a squeal.
And how the chicken, growing

limp, folds its
wings down around its breath
and gives up flight.
Suffering, then, is not

34

a dream from which any
of them ever wakes.
They will spill their lives
into the farmyard

and into the silence.
They will take the pain
somewhere where their tongues
cannot bother sound.

But I, the knife blade,
closer to them than anyone,
still write for eternity what
all blood must tell.

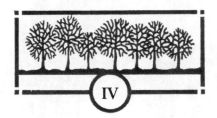

IV

THE WAY TO HELL

I am speaking now
with my tongues of fire.
I say to continue
in the direction you
were already heading.
Pave your road with sin
and you will find my place
at the end of it.
Give your life to wrongdoing,
to falsehood, and lies,
and I will promise
to use your bones for
the making of small kindling.
I will teach you of heat.
I will teach you the eternal
pain that makes
the nerves sing like birds
whose memory of happiness
has gone blind.
The souls here do not
remember either why north
differs from south,
or what argument made them
part, or what measure
time sends its sand to fall for.
That is why the sense
of direction could fail you
unless you fall in
with the company
of the murderers or thieves.
I apologize for any trouble
you have in finding me,
for the darkness, but all
the good here in the human
heart has burned out.

THE SQUIRRELS

It is the same for them.
They are instructed
in habits until
they see how a winter

waits behind the light.
In the shadow
of the falling leaves,
there is a path to the future.

They hurry and bury nuts
just to find it.
They are brown now
and come down from the trees.

They are brown and bend
their tasks
to the brown earth
and take to it

what needs to sleep
for a long time in darkness.
There they bury their
fear and chatter

and hide it in the earth's will.
To them a nut is
the promise to take them
through the season of death.

A BASKET OF BUTTONS

Lost eyes, whose sight
will not be restored.
What was there to see anyway?
You saw how the days
undid you.
You saw wear wear you out
and let you down, and how knots,
told to hold you, didn't.

It may be a disappointment,
but nothing turns out
as planned.

Perhaps the buttonhole you
left found another mate,
or the shirt itself
was torn up and now is
a rag that cleans dusty floors.

That is, nothing turns
out as planned.

Even blind now, you can
see that the needle will not
come back for you,
or stitch hope back
into your dreams. You
will sleep now in that basket
with the others who
do not belong anymore
to this world of work and play.

That is,
nothing, not even the fate
of one small
button, turns out as planned.

THE HUNTER

You want to kill.
The gun and axe you bring
were made for this.
They would die for this.

In the snow, blood
would open itself like a flower.
All the days are this day,
and time will not pass.

And the landscape holds
your desire for death
like another season, colder.
And the clues

to the animals run
before you as if to obey
and leave their partial speech.
It is your job to understand

their story, with
your gun to touch the secret
instant of a heartbeat
and leave it still.

The blackbirds will call
back and forth to one another,
but you will kill again.
All of this has been done

before by the others.
Murder like this is taught
or left to
the blind hands of instinct.

THIS IS THE SPARROW

This is the sparrow,
brown as the dust,
just a little chip of sound
that waters the silence.

Its bones so slight
they could still be ideas
that meekness had in mind.
Perhaps you think

that all a sparrow can do
is punctuate the flow of time
with its little life.
But this sparrow can sit

on a clean branch for you
in the heart of winter
when the cold is slowly taking
the world apart and the other

animals hide from pain
and when the wind has death
for its reasons.
This sparrow can go out

looking for the hard crumbs.
It already knows the question
that comes will ask
it to inherit the earth.

PLAYING DEAD

Who will write this poem?
Don't ask the silence.
It doesn't answer anyone.
Don't ask the alphabet, sound

asleep again.
Don't ask the pen.
It is out of thought and ink.
What will we write it with?

Don't ask the pencil either.
It has a broken point.
And the eraser can only erase.
If you asked it,

it would say that it wants
the world to disappear.
So how much can we say?
Ideas have wings and fly away.

There isn't much to say
about the lack of meaning.
I have a feeling that cleverness
never will show up.

Will it make us happy or sad?
Don't ask emptiness to smile.
In a poem without a message
every word is playing dead.

A PRAYER TO MY VOICE

I wanted to be a voice
that the words flocked to
like a frightened dusk.

I wanted to be a voice
that like a tree holds
their breath in its branches.

I wanted to be a place
that the words could call
the comfort of their story.

I wanted to tell of their
beginning and end,
full of dust and memory.

I wanted to see through
the thickness of meaning
to obscurity and ignorance.

I wanted to reach like the sun
into words and be
a night for their sleep.

And I would be their days,
and they would follow the life
of my road's thoughts.

And when I died, the words
I became would become
the skeletons of my breath.

TO KEEP YOU ALIVE

Hammer that built you
a house so you would not die
in the snow and cold.
Door that shut it.

Key that locked it.
Fire that warmed it and that
you brought dry twigs to
so that it would hiss

and keep the howling wolves away.
And fire that cooked
the meat and boiled the stew
so you would not die of hunger.

And floor that gathered
dirt your shoes brought in.
And broom that swept it out.
And water that washed away

the dirt of plates
so you would not die of sickness.
And cup that let you drink
so you would not die of thirst.

And even cloth that let you
wear it to keep the blood warm.
Or to sleep beneath so
moonlight would not chill the bones.

And even bed that let you
sleep up off the floor
so the cold of the dead
was not what you dreamt about.

44

H IS FOR HORROR

See on the platform
of the H the hangman waiting,
and the blindfolded one
led up the two stairs.
See how the O of the noose
is pulled shut.
See how the O of the hanged
one's mouth falls open
when his last breath
goes out for good.
And then he sort of slumps
like an R, no, like two R's,
hanging as they would
by their own dead weight.
R's with little serif feet
that dangle.
No need to wash those
feet anymore, or trim
the nails, or buy
the shoes that fit them.
And when the hanged one
is taken down
out of the air, see how
heavy he is, like a bag of bones.
But no, this bag is full
of cold blood, and the O
in that blood will not roll
back and forth.
And what of the last R
in horror, you will say?
And I will say, don't ask me.
Ask the jury, the judge,
and the jailor, who are
so good at thinking up
the darkest sentences.

MY GRAVEYARD POEM

Plenty of melancholy.
The little plots
so neatly trimmed because
the dead like it that way.

And the pots of flowers
that perk up the scene
with their need to bloom.
And a few birds, the first

visitors, to break the solitude.
Let them perch and peck.
They seem to be the only
ones not so afraid

of one or two ghosts.
And the caretaker, who makes
the rounds, for whom
time has not yet stopped.

All those who doze
in their underground beds
cannot dream the world back.
Only the granite headstone,

cold and leaning, comes close.
And on it those markings
that shrink life
to the pause between two

dates, so that everything
here has been settled, like
addition or subtraction,
whichever way you look at it.

46

THE WOLF

In winter the wolf
lets its hair grow thicker.
Thick as a bush
unaware of its thorns.

And the coat grows darker,
the way the meaning
of a shadow falls
deeper into the darkness
of the mind and fear starts
its own season.

Then the wind sharpens
the wolf's teeth the way
hunger does.
A rabbit in the mind
always runs before
the appetite to prepare it.
Or a sparrow that pretends
it is a random leaf
and flutters bare song.

But there is never enough
for the wolf to eat.
And when its snout and ears
think for it, it will
make tracks that trick
the snow and go unsolved.

The wolf's mind
is the answer, hunts and
turns to the directions
only known by an evil heart.
The wolf's heart
is the only reason why
there is so little good left
on this earth.

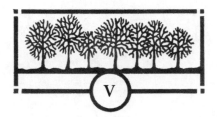

V

SHADOW, COME CLOSE

Shadow, come close
and listen to all I tell.
It's true
that you and I were born

out of the same darkness
to share the same
shape and the same soul.
We were both given breath

to play with and time
to beat inside of us,
and made to walk together
through this world of light,

where my eyes do the looking.
But it isn't true what
the others think, that you
were only made to follow.

We are one and you are
mine and I am yours.
And when I give up this weight
of bones and skin I wear,

it will be your job again
to lead us both back
to that complete darkness
from which we came.

51

CAT IN THE CORNER

You invite sleep to
curl up with you,
and you two forget the hours.
Time passes beyond your
dreams, the twitch
of your whiskers.
Time almost forgets you.
Perhaps you sleep because
you dream of distance
and mice that run
on to infinity,
and you enjoy the pleasure
of never catching them.
To wake you would break
back into the hurt of time,
the stop and start of need.
But even now, you pause
to breathe, to reach
back again for air
in the world you have left,
to show you still
do belong to the living.
And here, before us,
eyes closed, you stir, you
move your sleeping shoulders
and rest your chin.
Cat in the corner,
you are not the only one
who has stretched the mind.
You are not the only master
of that darker world
and the bright, waking one,
choosing whenever you want
to enter one or both.

KEEP ON PRAYING

Little words on wings,
on your way up
through the cosmos,
past the secrets of the stars

you will go until
you bring back an answer.
All our hopes and fears
go up with you.

And all our heavy troubles,
knotted on this earth,
rooted in our mortality, fly.
To be human, we know

the ache of bone and blood,
the ties of time
that lead us on like
heavy animals to the gravity

of the grave.
Out of the heavy mouths.
Out of the heavy books,
only you, little prayers,

know how to fly,
how to make language so light
that each vowel
and syllable patters

on the infinite brain there,
telling it the elaborate
plan of pain,
and to please release us.

ONE

How many poets does it
take to write this poem?
One to empty out the pockets
of her dreams.
One to sleep on it.
One to stick her toe into
the river of her thoughts.
One to pick the bone
of her memory.
One to look into her heart
and dip the pen.
One to call in misery for company.
One to hit the nail
of punctuation on the head.
One to look truth in the eye.
One to crack the nut
of the skull to find meaning.
One to chase away
the other cooks of the stew.
One to grind the axe of logic.
One with the two heads
that are better than one.
One with the fine words
that butter no bread.
One to stand on her soapbox.
One to complain and split
the hairs of imperfection.
One to say the rotten apple
is the first to fall
off the tree.
One to read it aloud to
the ill wind that blows no good.
One to say, shut up, you fools.
Leave it alone now.
This poor flogged poem is
as good as finished.

NEEDLEWORK

Help is on the way.
I am the needle
of starlight and wind.
I am the silver one like them,
and when you pull me
out of your pin cushion,
I will fly for you.
I will fly when the thread,
licked by spit until it points,
threads my eye.
And then I will see forward.
And the thread and I
will not look back to
that unwinding
of time off the spool.
But the two of us, like
a body and its shadow, will
fly over the miles of cloth
to the hems, the darts,
and the cuffs in need,
and there we will work for you
the trickery of the stitch
that holds the far near.
And there in time
we will save what comes undone
and the bare threads
that were ready to give up.
And we will leave behind
the knots like roots
to hold all our good works
in place.
I am the needle and fly,
and I stitch what I preach.
And this is my creed:
to make your salvation
the thread of my thought.

A ROLLING PIN POEM

Now you are the creator.
Make any shape
out of this heap of dough,
a face to look at you,
a body with limbs.

Or flatten it
to fit a pan, and fill it
with the red of berries,
picked deep in the woods
where the bears prowl.

Just roll the dough out
and make it behave.
It isn't wheat in a field
anymore, and you
are not the gentle wind
that makes the grains nod
and dream of eternity.

Wake this dough up
and make it mortal and roll
it out to east and west
and make it reach.
And sprinkle it with more
flour so it doesn't
dare to stick or hold back.

Soon this dough will be
as thin as skin and
you will see the shape of
your plans behind it.
Then lay it down in the pan.
Then you are mighty,
and what you create is good.

THE PULL OF GRAVITY

This could be gravity.
This could be
the mind in rock talking.
The speed of these

particles could now
invisibly keep you here.
This could be earth.
I could be practicing my will.

Mountains bring me
their sullen blue and a
lightning strikes.
I could be pulling you,

your breath and your bones.
I could be pulling you,
the way earth makes
an apple want to fall.

What is my strength
but in my voice and how you
listen to what I say?
Listen to me.

I am what the roots want
for you, and blind worms.
This is how, finally,
the dead accomplish a voice.

JOKES

Why did the chicken
cross to
the other side of the road?
Because it wanted to get

to the other side.
That is why the cow
in the field jumped the fence
for grass. Why the pig,

fat on eating, got out
and ate all the farmer's
corn down to bare cob.
Why the horse, quick to catch

on, ran out of the red barn.
Why the horse,
because it loved jokes too,
trampled the fair wheat.

And why else,
except for laughter, did
the dog wag its tail and bark,
and wake up the farmer

from his deep sleep?
And make the farmer, in his
house, look out
and laugh to see his wise

and foolish animals destroy
his farm. Just for the sake
of wit, just to joke
on the way to the cold grave.

THE DANCE OF DEATH

I am death and dance.
I dance the earth flat.
The grave is my drum,
and beneath it
the bones roll and rattle.
The miller hears my dance
above the slow
grinding of his wheat.
The wheels of water and stone
turn to make a flour
that ends in bread.
But the miller knows his
end and that his last
dance belongs to me.
And the merchant, too,
above the clink and clank
of his gold coins, hears it.
However full he fills
his pockets, the pounding
of my feet is louder
than the tick of time.
And heard, even in the spring,
by the peasant ploughing
a furrow into the field,
and by the beggar, the king,
the pope, and the whore.
The tailor stitches torn
cloth, and the cook stirs
a spoon in the boiling stew,
but I am death, and my dance
outwhirls the wind
and the fury of the fire.
I dance to the music of war,
pestilence, and pain.
And so that you, too, hear it,
I dance these words
on the floor of your ear.

THIS SCARECROW

You made this scarecrow.
You nailed the bones
together and hung on them
the worn-out hat and shirt.

All summer this
skeleton of wood haunted.
It scared above the square
world of the garden.

It shook its wind-blown arms,
so that the crows,
those dark thieves,
would not fly in to peck

the seeds to death.
And the buried seeds woke
out of earth and reached
for light, and when they

were done again lay
down the heads of their new
seeds so they could sleep.
But now it is so cold,

and this scarecrow that scared
so well, that scared
away the dark plots
of the crows against life,

cannot scare away winter.
And this scarecrow stares
above the dead garden because
you do not take it down.

BONE SOUP

Here's a soup to
fight the wicked chill.
Bones that give up
the flavor of their souls.
Bones that cannot remember
what body held them
together for a life.

Chicken, pig, or cow?
The only answer bubbles
its breath above the flame.
And identity doesn't
matter when the wind
still seeks more victims.

You can stir the bones
to rattle against
the pot, as if to say,
death is not peaceful here.
That is how the eulogy
thickens, sprinkled
with parsley and salt.

Taste is what you came for.
Hunger keeps gnawing
on your body as
long as time will last.

Take some of this bone
soup to fill your bowl.
Spoon it to your mouth.
The bones are passing on to
you, life to life.
That is the final sacrament.